Basic Investing Guide For The New Investor

Basic Investing Guide For The New Investor

2nd Edition, Updated

Alfred V. Scillitani

Writers Club Press

San Jose New York Lincoln Shanghai

Basic Investing Guide For The New Investor
2nd Edition, Updated

Writers Club Press
an imprint of iUniverse, Inc.

For information address:
iUniverse, Inc.
5220 S. 16th St., Suite 200
Lincoln, NE 68512
www.iuniverse.com

This guide contains opinions and ideas of its author. If the reader requires personal assistance or advice, a professional financial planner should be consulted. Prior performance of an investment does not guarantee future results. Read fund prospectus before investing.

ISBN: 0-595-21183-6

Printed in the United States of America

DEDICATION

I would like to dedicate this book to my wife Crystal and son Matthew. I would also like to dedicate to this book to everyone just starting out and trying to invest.

CONTENTS

Foreword

There are thousands of investment books and guides to help people. They cover things like investing in stocks, options, futures, selling short, bonds, CD's, and hundreds of other investment options. After reading all 400 pages of these "easy to understand" books you are more confused about investing then you were before. This guide will help you get the basic understanding of how to invest for your retirement and give you the confidence to start.

INTRODUCTION

This is the 2nd Edition to the popular book "Basic Investing Guide For The New Investor, Start Investing With As Little As $50 Per Month." This edition includes all of the easy to understand investment information from the first edition, updates and new rules for retirement investing in the years 2002 and beyond, information on popular Exchange Traded Funds, investment definitions, and more.

Like the first edition, this guide will give you the information you need to help you start investing for your retirement. Every year that passes by represents thousands of dollars lost for you in your retirement years. You need to start now and all it takes is as little as $50 per month.

BUDGETING

After speaking with people about investing, I realized that budgeting was almost always a factor. Many people are literally wasting hundreds of dollars every month on things they do not need. Purchasing expensive items without shopping around, going out to eat 3 or 4 times a week, making spontaneous purchases...I can go on forever. Budgeting starts with a plan.

You want to start putting money away regularly for your retirement, but how? You do not have much to spare? Start with as little as $50 per month. The important thing is to start NOW!!! Every year that passes by may cost you thousands of dollars.

Later in this guide I will discuss compounding, but let me give you a taste of what compounding is. Let's say you are 30 years old and have the ability to save $50 per month. You are thinking $50 per month, big deal. If you add $50 per month for 30 years (you would be 60 years old), your total investment would only be $18,000. Now let's compound. The stock market has been averaging just over 13%. If you invested your $50 a month at age 30, in a mutual fund averaging 13% for 30 years your $18,000 would be worth over $215,000. No, that is not a typo, your $50 per month would be worth $215,000.

Are you having trouble coming up with the extra $50 per month?

Review your day. You wake up, get dressed for work, stop on the way to work to get a cup of coffee ($2/day), buy lunch at a fast food restaurant

($5/day), come home exhausted so you eat out ($60/week), have a glass of soda/beer ($10/week), and go to bed.

> *Coffee $2/day = $60 per month (daily)
> *Lunch $5/day = $100 per month (5 days a week)
> *Eat dinner out twice a week = $60 per week = $240 per month
> *Soda or beer/wine = $10 per week = $40 per month
> *Do you smoke? If you do, $20 per week = $80 per month

Grand total = $520 per month. I am sure you can find other items to add to this list.

Where Is Your Money Going?

One of the best ways to track your expenses is to write them all down on a sheet of paper. Use your checkbook as a guide. First write down your fixed monthly expenses (rent/mortgage, car payment, insurance, etc...). After your fixed expenses, write down your expenses that vary (phone average $50 per month, utilities average $80 per month, etc...).

Expenses per month	*Income* per month
Rent $500	
Car $200	Household income is
Insurance $100	$35,000 per year.
Gas $60	After taxes, take home
Food $300	pay is $2,275 per month.
Cable $80	
Utilities $80	
Phones $50	
$1,370	$2,275

Subtract your expenses from your income ($2275-$1370) and the remainder is your extra income ($905) per month. Where is this "extra" income going? Chances are the money is not going anywhere special. When you track your expenses from your check book you will see $25 spent here, $17 spent there, $62 here, $22 there. All of those little purchases add up to your "extra" income.

The next step is to review your expenses and determine where you can cut back. Even if you do not have "extra" income, you can see how easy it is to save $50 or more every month. If your cable bill is $80 per month, you need to decide if you really need 200 channels. Simply cutting back in this one area can leave you with an extra $50 per month.

Things you can do right now to save more money

Make a weekly food menu and buy only the items needed for the week. Possible savings—$20 per week, $80 per month

Change long distance companies. Go on the internet, shop around. There are companies, like Bigzoo.com, that charge only a few pennies per minute. Possible savings—$10 to $70 per month

Shop around for expensive items like furniture, cars, car tires, even sneakers. Do not wait until you have to purchase these items. Start your search at least one month before these items are needed. Ask your friends if they know of any good deals. Again, the internet is a great resource. I bought new tires for my car online and saved about $150 including installation. Possible savings—thousands per year

Call your credit card company and ask for a lower rate. That's right, simply ask for a lower rate. A few percentage points can save you a lot of money. Possible savings—hundreds monthly (depending on amount owed)

Saving starts with discipline. Make a budget, stick to it, and have the money that you want to invest deposited directly into the investments from your payroll or bank account. Now that you know you have the money to invest, let's get started!

DEBT MANAGEMENT

The first step in reducing debt is to find out how you got into debt. Are you purchasing items that you do not need? Are you buying items without checking other stores for better prices? Once you find out the cause of your debt, you will be able start reducing your debt.

Reducing Debt

Reducing your debt is a slow and painful process. Write down all of your credit card debt and interest rates of each card on a sheet of paper. You can combine all of your bills onto your lowest interest rate card then call the company to try to get the interest rate lowered. Sometimes a phone call is all that it takes. Interest rates on credit cards range from 9.99% fixed to a variable rate over 21%. If your card is over 15%, call the credit card company and ask if they would lower the rate. If you have received an offer in the mail from another credit card company with a lower rate, let them know. Nicely tell them that you received an offer from another company for a lower rate card, but would prefer to stay with them. Ask if they can match the rate. If your company refuses to lower your rate, check magazines, the internet, and newspapers for a lower interest rate credit card to switch to.

If you feel you need professional help, there are debt consolidation companies that will help you. Search for non-profit organizations first and get references. Make sure you compare fee's (if any).

Investing and Reducing Debt?

You may be able to invest and reduce debt at the same time. If your debt is under control and your interest rate on your credit card is 10% or less you may decide to pay off your credit card and start investing at the same time. Take the amount you are paying over your minimum and cut it in half. Keep paying off your credit card with the minimum plus the extra half and invest the other half. If your minimum payment is $150 and you have been giving $250, cut the extra $100 in half and give $50 to the credit card company ($200 total) and $50 to your investments.

If your credit card interest rate is 11% or higher and you cannot get it lowered, keep giving the extra cash to your credit card. Why? It is all about percentages. The stock market is averaging about 13% per year. If your credit card interest rate is lower than 11%, you can start investing at the same time. If your interest rate is 11% or higher, which is higher than the stock market average, you would be losing money if you invested it unless your invested money beat the credit card rate.

EMERGENCY FUND

Before you start investing for your retirement, you must have an emergency fund (e-fund). You need to have easy accessible cash in case of unexpected emergencies: lose your job, car breaks down, home repairs, etc…The e-fund should consist of 1 to 5 months of your monthly salary. The size of your e-fund depends on your family size, your obligations, your job security, and how quickly you feel you can become employed again at your current salary if you lose your job.

Start your e-fund in a local banks Money Market Account (MMA). Shop around for the best interest rates. A MMA usually has higher interest rates than a typical savings account and you can remove funds from the MMA very rapidly if you need them. If your banks MMA minimum initial investment is too high, start saving money in your banks savings account. Once your savings account contains the amount of money you need to start a MMA, transfer the e-fund into the banks Money Market Account

DOLLAR COST AVERAGING
AND COMPOUNDING

Dollar Cost Averaging is investing the same amount of money at regular intervals. You reduce your average cost per share over time because you buy more shares when the price is lower.

Mutual Fund Price	Monthly Purchase Amount	Number of Share's Bought
$13	$50	3.85
$14	$50	3.57
$15	$50	3.33
$13	$50	3.85
$15	$50	3.33
$18	$50	2.78
$12	$50	4.17
$13	$50	3.85
$17	$50	2.94

Notice, when the mutual fund price is lower you purchase more shares with your $50 than when the price is higher.

Once you figure out how much you can invest each month, have the mutual fund company withdraw the funds directly from your payroll or bank account. You will have the option to do this when you initially set up an account. You can increase, decrease, or stop the automatic payments at anytime.

How Compounding Works

Compounding is what happens to money at various interest rates over time. One example mentioned earlier was $50/month at 13% interest for 30 years. The total investment was only $18,000, but because of compounding, the $18,000 becomes $215,000. Here is another example of compounding to help you understand how a small amount of money can grow:

I give you $1 and tell you every year you will double your money. Day 1 = $1; 2 = $2; 3 = $4…day 10 = $512; day 15 = $16,384; day 20 = $524,288. The longer you compound your funds, the more dramatic the increases. The earlier you start to invest, the easier it is to accumulate wealth.

The Story of Bob and Slob

Let me tell you the story of twins Bob and Slob. Bob gets his first full-time job at age 20 and decides to immediately start investing. He opens a Roth IRA and starts investing into a mutual fund. He invests $166 per month ($2,000 per year) into the mutual fund, which is averaging 13% per year. Bob does this for 10 years. At age 30, Bob decides to stop investing. Slob also gets his first full-time job at age 20. Slob decides to buy a nice car, expensive jewelry, and expensive electronic games instead of investing right away. At age 30, Slob realizes he must start investing so he starts to invest $166 per month ($2,000 a year) into a Roth IRA mutual fund averaging 13% per year. Slob invests $166 per month not for 10 years, but for the next 30 years. At age 60, guess who has more money? I'll give you a hint…It's not Slob! Slob would have approximately $725,000; Bob would have over 1.2 million dollars. Compounding!!!

Quick Trick: Rule of 72

The Rule of 72 states that you can determine how long it will take to double your money by dividing 72 by a given interest rate.

At 10% interest, your money will double in 7.2 years. 72 divided by 10= 7.2 At 12% interest, 6 years. 72 divided by 12= 6. At 2% interest (possibly your savings account rate?), 36 years!!!

ASSET ALLOCATION AND DIVERSIFICATION

"Don't put all your eggs in one basket," your risk of losing everything greatly increases. If you invested $12,000 in XYZ company in May of 1999 at $60 per share, you would own 200 shares ($60/share, $12,000 invested). In February of 2000, the company you invested in gets audited and numerous discrepancies are found. The stock drops to $14 per share. Your $12,000 investment is now worth $2800. If you think I am exaggerating, think again. The above scenario actually happened to a very large, well-respected company called Waste Management (stock symbol WMI). It happens all the time. Leave the individual stock picking to the experienced professional. Diversifying, having a proper asset allocation, and investing in mutual funds will reduce your risk significantly.

Risk Tolerance

You must determine your risk tolerance before you start investing. There is a direct link between the risk you are willing to take, and the return on your investments. The higher your risk tolerance, usually the higher your returns.

In October 1987, stocks fell by 20% in a single day. If you were investing long-term and the investment you owned fell over 20% in a very short period of time, what would you do? Would you sell all of the investment? Sell a portion of the investment? Do nothing? Buy more of the investment? This is a question you must ask yourself. The stock market is not a sure thing. Investing for the long term decreases your risks and increases your wealth. Everyone's risk tolerance is different, which means everyone's asset allocation will be different.

You should start with a basic allocation. The asset allocation you set up today will change over time because your accounts will grow at different rates and your tolerances may change as you become more comfortable with investing. After investing for several years, you may want to add International Funds and Growth Funds. I discuss these funds in Chapter 10.

If you are just starting out and have 30 or more years until retirement, this is what a basic allocation might look like:

Aggressive Investor	*Moderate Investor*	*Conservative Investor*
100% Stock Mutual Funds (Avg. 10% to 15% return)	70% Stock Mutual Funds 30% Non-stock Holdings (Avg. 8% to 13% return)	50% Stock Mutual Funds 50% Non-stock Holdings (Avg. 5% to 10% return)

Your Non-stock Holdings can be anything from a bond mutual fund to a savings account at your local bank.

MUTUAL FUNDS

A mutual fund is a group of stocks, bonds, or cash combined in numerous ways and sold as shares. When you invest in a mutual fund, your money is combined with the money of others. For example: An **Index 500 Fund** holds shares of stock from 500 of the largest U.S. companies (Microsoft, Exxon, IBM, Walmart, etc...). It is designed to provide investors with a broad exposure to the large capitalization sector of the U.S. Market. Each mutual fund share contains a piece of each stock. If you own one share of an Index 500 Fund, you own a piece of all 500 companies. It is an efficient diversification tool. Index funds are also tax efficient. Stocks within the fund are rarely traded, so capital gains taxes (discussed later) are minimal and fees remain low. An Index 500 fund should be the core of your portfolio.

Three other funds I would like to discuss are the Total Stock Market Index Funds, Life Strategy Funds, and Exchange Traded Funds.

The Total Stock Market Index Fund invests in all U.S. stocks (currently over 7,000). This fund is similar to the Index 500 fund, but is even more diversified because it invests in large, medium, and small sized companies.

Life Strategy Funds are becoming very popular. Mutual fund companies are starting these types of funds because they are almost maintenance free for the investor. You usually have a choice of life funds, one for growth, one for moderate growth, and one for the conservative investor. The fund manager allocates a certain percent of your money into stocks, bonds, and cash. You do not have to do anything. Pick your current risk, high (growth), medium (moderate), low (conservative) and change funds as you get closer to retirement.

Exchange Traded Funds (ETF) can track the performance of a growing number of different index funds. Most ETF's represent a portfolio of stocks designed to track one specific index. ETF's can be bought and sold exactly like a stock of an individual company during the entire trading day. The major benefits of ETF's are the low expenses (like index funds) and tax benefits. With a regular mutual fund, other investors selling the fund can force managers to sell stocks in order to meet redemption's, which can result in taxable capital-gains distributions being sent to shareholders (you). This is not the case with ETF's, you own it like a single stock. ETF's have no minimum investment. However, every time you buy or sell an ETF, you pay a brokerage commission. If you are planning to contribute money monthly to your fund, ETF's may end up costing more because of the commissions.

Mutual Fund Expenses

Another reason why Index and Life Funds are great is due to low expenses. Many managed funds, which trade in and out of stocks frequently, pay a fund manager to research these stocks. Expenses and commissions can range from .18 percent (many index funds) to over 6 percent (many commission based fund companies). These percents do not look like much, but let us add the **power of compounding:**

> *Index 500 Fund returns 13%, subtract .6% in expenses, total 12.4%. If you invested $1000 right now at 12.4% and left it for 30 years, it would be worth $33,340.

*XYZ managed fund returns 13% also, subtract 3% for expenses, total 10%. If you invested $1000 right now at 10% and left it for 30 years, it would be worth $17,450.

Absolutely amazing what a few percentage points can do over time! How can Index Funds charge so little? They are considered "unmanaged" funds. Yes, there is a fund manager and he or she monitors the stocks and money flow. With most Index Funds, the fund manager invests half of the total amount of money they are given equally among all the stocks in the index. The manager then invests the other half in, what they feel, are undervalued companies within the index. They rarely sell shares of stock within the index and they do not have to research stocks outside of the index, so fees are low.

Prospectus

One of the first things you need to do before investing in mutual fund is read the funds prospectus. A mutual fund company must inform you to read their Prospectus before investing, but what is a prospectus?

A **Prospectus** is an offer to sell shares of a mutual fund. You are required to read the prospectus before investing because it contains pertinent information regarding the fund and the risks of the fund.

Topics the Prospectus should include:
Funds Goals: Does the fund invest in growth stocks or is it interested in stocks that produce income?

Funds Strategies: What is the fund's Asset Allocation and Diversification? What percent of the fund is invested in cash? What is the greatest percent the manager can invest in any one company? What is the fund manager's theory on deciding which stocks to buy or sell?

Operating Expenses and Fee's: Does the fund have a load (sales commission) or is it no-load? What are the operating expenses charged by the fund company? Are there any fee's or charges for withdrawing your money (redemption fees)?

Fund Manager(s): Who is running the fund? What is the manager's experience? How long have they been managing this fund? What is their financial experience?

Risks Involved: The prospectus should discuss the risks of investing. Your investment is not guaranteed. The fact that you can loose money. The phrase that you will always see, "the fund's past performance does not represent how it will perform in the future." In other words, just because the fund returned 25% last year, does not mean it will return 25% this year.

The prospectus should also include general information about the mutual fund company and policies:
What is the funds minimum initial investment? How can you buy and sell shares of the fund? How to contact the company? Special services and other information about the fund.

Planning to buy that mutual fund outside of an Individual Retirement Account (IRA) or Employer Sponsored Account (401k)? You need to check two things:

a) What is the funds history of capital gains distributions? Your taxable fund (outside of any retirement accounts) may have a history of high turnover (the manager trades frequently). This means high tax consequences for you.

b) When are you planning on buying the fund? Check the funds capital gains distribution date. If you buy the fund in October and the distribution date is November, you will have to pay taxes on ALL of the gains as if you owned the fund for the entire year. A capital gain is when the fund manager sells a stock in the fund for a profit. The profit (gain) is distributed to the shareholders. The shareholders will have to pay taxes on the distribution. For example: you buy a mutual fund at $40 per share. The mutual fund distributes a $4 per share gain to its shareholders. The share price will drop by the distribution amount ($40 per share will drop to $36) and the shareholder pays tax on the $4 per share. If you purchase the fund before the distribution record date, you will pay taxes on the distribution as if you had the fund all year. There is not a required month that all mutual funds must distribute their capital gains. However, most distribute their gains October through December. If you purchase shares in September and the funds distribution date is in October, you may end up paying capital gains on that fund for the entire tax year even though you had the fund only one month. What to do? Call or e-mail the fund company and ask for the distribution record date for that specific fund. Make sure you ask for the earliest date that you can purchase the shares without paying the capital gains for the current year.

Employer-Sponsored Retirement Accounts

Employer-sponsored retirement accounts like a 401k and 403b are plans set up by your employer for you to use for your retirement funds. These funds are not to be withdrawn until age 59 1/2. You usually have an option of which funds to invest in. Which fund(s) should you invest in? The fund(s) you invest in are based on many factors:

Your Risk Tolerance

Do you feel comfortable with the ups and downs of the stock market? The more aggressively you invest the higher volatility of your portfolio. Retirement accounts are used for your long-term funds. You should be more aggressive in these accounts.

Are you planning to invest outside of your 401k and IRA?

Why is this question important? Taxes! Let's say that you are planning to invest in a growth fund, international fund, and an index fund. Most growth and international funds trade stocks within the fund frequently, which means higher capital gains taxes for you to pay. Index funds trade infrequently, so capital gains taxes are minimal. Have the growth fund in your tax-deferred account and the index fund in your taxable account. Yes, you can have index funds in your tax-deferred accounts. You can have as many funds as you want in your account(s) as long as you do not exceed the maximum contribution limits.

Example:

You invest the maximum to your 401k $11,000. You invest the maximum to your IRA $3,000. You invest $1,000 to a mutual fund outside of your 401k and IRA. Total $15,000. Your asset allocation may look like this:

In your 401k: $2,000 International fund, $9,000 Index fund (Total $11,000)
In your IRA: $2000 Growth fund, $1000 Index 500 fund (Total $3,000)
In your taxable account: $1,000 Index 500 fund

What options do you have? Index funds, growth funds, international funds, etc...

Each company plan is different. You may have a very limited choice of mutual funds or you may have hundreds to choose from. Choose based on your risk tolerance. Most plans let you change funds whenever you want. Start conservatively if you wish then change later to a more aggressive approach. The main issue is to get started.

Talk to your benefits department (or your 401k representative), that's what they are there for. The best part of an employer-sponsored plan is that most companies contribute funds to match your contributions (up to a certain limit).

Most plans are worded as such: the company will match up to 50% of your contributions, not to exceed 3% of your salary. In other words, if you invest 6% of your salary, they will contribute 3% (50% of your 6%). If you contribute 8%, they still contribute 3% (max. 3%). If you contribute 4%, they will contribute 2% (50% of your contribution).

A question often asked is whether or not to invest in a company's 401k or a Roth IRA?

The 401k, up to the company match, should be utilized first. If you have extra money to invest, start a Roth IRA. If you have more money to invest (good for you) after your 401k company match and contributing the maximum to your Roth IRA, then go back to your 401k and invest more. Ask your benefits department for your 401k maximum contributions (usually 10% to 20% of your salary).

Should you take advantage of this benefit? YES!!! It's free money. If you invest 6% of your $30,000 salary, your first benefit is that the 6% ($1,800) is withdrawn before taxes. Instead of your $30,000 getting taxed, you pay taxes on $28,200. The second benefit is the free money. They contribute 3% ($900). You invested $1,800; they invested $900 for a total of $2700 in one year. That's a 50% return on your money. You just lowered your taxes and received a $900 bonus for your retirement. Start now!!!

Year 2002 and beyond maximums for your 401k, 403b, and 457 plans

2002	2003	2004	2005	2006	2007*
$11,000	$12,000	$13,000	$14,000	$15,000	$15,000

*Starting 2007, inflation adjustments of $500 are added to maximums

Individual Retirement Accounts (IRA's)

Myth: An IRA is a type of Mutual Fund
Fact: An IRA is an account that you put a mutual fund (or other invest-
ment) into for retirement purposes.

Maximums for year 2002 and beyond for your IRA

2002	2003	2004	2005	2006	2007
$3,000	$3,000	$3,000	$4,000	$4,000	$4,000

*Starting 2008, increase to $5,000 and inflation adjustments of $500 are
added to maximums yearly

There are 2 types of retirement IRA's: Traditional and the Roth. I will
briefly cover the Traditional IRA. The only time you may want to look into
the Traditional IRA is if you are within a few years of retirement and you
will remain in a 15% tax bracket. The Roth IRA usually works out to be
your best bet, especially if you are young and just starting out. However,
you must use earned income to contribute to either of these IRA's.

The Traditional IRA is a retirement account. You choose the mutual
fund(s) you want to invest in for your retirement. The fund(s) you choose
comprise your Traditional IRA. You can deduct contributions into your
Traditional IRA if you are not *eligible* during any part of the year to partic-
ipate in a company plan. If you are eligible to contribute to a company
plan, you still may not be able to deduct your contribution. You must be at

or below a certain income level to qualify for full deductions. Once you reach the income level set for that year, your allowed deduction starts to fade out until you are no longer permitted to deduct your contribution. The income limit changes, so check with the mutual fund company for the current year's limits. The main disadvantage to the Traditional IRA is that fact that your money is taxed when you start withdrawing your money.

The Roth IRA is a retirement account. You choose the mutual fund(s) you want to invest in for your retirement. The fund(s) you choose comprise your Roth IRA. Here is a summary of the Roth IRA:

> *You can have as many Roth IRA's as you like, but you still cannot contribute more than the yearly maximum to all of the IRA's combined (refer to previous chart for yearly maximums).

> *Contributions by a non-working spouse are also allowed up to maximum.

> *There is no age limit on contributions.

> *Your adjusted gross income (AGI) must be less than $160,000 for joint filers and $110,000 for a single filer to make the maximum contribution. (These limits may change yearly. There is also a phase out range. If you are near this amount of income, contact the mutual fund company for phase out limits).

> *Your AGI must be less than $100,000 to convert from a Traditional IRA to a Roth IRA. Be aware, you will owe taxes on the conversion.

*Contributions are not tax-deductible.

*Participation in an employer's retirement plan does not affect your ability to qualify for a Roth IRA.

*Qualified distributions are not allowed in the first five years.

*Distributions are not required until the owner's death.

*After five years, the entire distribution is nontaxable for an owner over age 59 1/2, or a qualified first home purchase (up to $10,000), or if the owner dies, or is disabled.

*Qualified distributions, including earnings, are **nontaxable**. Not only is the Roth IRA tax deferred (you do not have to pay taxes each year on the money in the IRA), it is also nontaxable (you do not have to pay taxes on the money you withdraw for your retirement).

*Withdrawals can also be taken penalty-free at any time if they are used to pay for higher education expenses. There are also additional circumstances where funds from a Roth IRA can be used without penalty, including death, disability, medical expenses, or if the investor uses a series of substantially equal periodic payments. These situations would apply even if the Roth IRA has been in existence for less than five years.

THE BASIC PORTFOLIO

The first few years of your portfolio may not look very motivating, but do not get discouraged. Remember, you must start with an emergency fund. Once your e-fund is complete, invest in your company's sponsored plan, then start a Roth IRA. Invest in an Index 500 Fund, Total Stock Market Index Fund, Life Strategy Fund, or ETF. You may add more aggressive growth funds as your risk tolerance increases. Recommended mutual fund companies are listed in the appendix.

This is a sample portfolio of someone just starting out. Managed Growth and International Funds are not included in this portfolio. The portfolio is assuming a 13% rate of return on the Index 500 mutual fund and 5% return on the e-fund. The portfolio is also assuming the investor is 25 years old, has a salary of $30,000, an established emergency fund of $2,500, and is initially contributing $50 per month to a Roth IRA.

*Asset allocation and growth, investing 1-10 years.

Year	Fund	Amount	Percent of Portfolio
1	E-fund	$2,600	80.5%
	Mutual Fund	$630	19.5%

Total Amount Invested $3,230

*After 3rd year, person increases contribution to $150 per month

Year	Fund	Amount	Percent of Portfolio
3	E-fund	$2,900	57.7%
	Mutual Fund	$2,125	42.3%

Total Amount Invested $5,025

Year	Fund	Amount	Percent of Portfolio
5	E-fund	$3,200	32.3%
	Mutual Fund	$6,700	67.7%

Total Amount Invested $9,900

Year	Fund	Amount	Percent of Portfolio
10	E-fund	$4,000	15.6%
	Mutual Fund	$21,600	84.4%

Total Amount Invested $25,600 (at this point you are 35 years old)

**Asset allocation and growth, investing 11-30 years:

Year	Fund	Amount	Percent of Portfolio
20	E-fund	$6,600	5.7%
	Mutual Fund	$110,000	94.3%

Total Amount Invested $116,000 (45 years old)

As you approach retirement start adding bonds to your portfolio. They are safer investment tools. Again, usually the safer the investment, the lower the returns. Add 2% bonds (or bond fund) for every year you are over 45. After 20 years, age 65, you may want to stop adding bonds to your portfolio. You may live to age 85, so you still need your money to grow as you get older.

Year	Fund	Amount	Percent of Portfolio
30	E-fund	$10,800	3.3%
	Bond	$65,000	20%
Mutual Fund		$250,000	76.7%

Total Amount Invested $325,800 (55 years old)

READY TO ADD MANAGED GROWTH AND INTERNATIONAL FUNDS?

Which Managed Growth or International Funds should you choose? Here is a concise list of items to look for:

Determine Your Needs and Risk Tolerance.

If you are invested in an Index 500 fund you may want to add a U.S. stock fund that invests in small or mid-sized companies, or find an International fund (invests in companies primarily outside of the U.S.). The Index 500 fund invests in large capitalization companies (value of company's shares outstanding is over $5 billion). To diversify, you want to find a fund that does not duplicate your current funds holdings. Most small capitalization (shares outstanding $100 million to $500 million) funds are aggressive growth funds. The share price of a small capitalization fund will increase and decrease dramatically. These funds are not for the low risk, conservative investor. International funds invest in U.S. and foreign companies. International funds come with risk also, but they are a good diversification tool. If the U.S. economy starts to decline, foreign countries may become more appealing to investors. Money will flow into those foreign countries increasing their value and, in turn, increasing their stock prices.

Fund Expenses.

Once you find a fund you like, compare it with similar funds. You may find two or more funds that invest in the same stocks with similar returns.

One of the funds may have much lower expenses then the other. The lower the expenses, the more money you get to keep for your retirement. Use the Mutual Fund Review Forms in Appendix D.

Consistency.

With managed funds, review returns for 5 years or longer (if possible). Look for consistency and average returns higher than funds investing in similar companies.

Manager Tenure.

How long has the manager been with the fund? The 5 year return may not mean much if the fund company hired a new manager last week.

How To Set-up An Account With A Mutual Fund Company

It is very easy to start an account once you know the fund company and the specific fund you wish to invest in. If you do not have a computer with access to the internet, turn to Appendix C for phone numbers and minimum initial investments.

If you do have access to the internet, just go to Basicinvest.com or search for other financial websites (there are thousands). The Mutual Funds section of Basicinvest has direct links to several well respected mutual fund companies. The company's minimum initial investments are listed on the website to save you hours of searching time. Find the fund companies that meet your minimums and click on their links. If you find a fund that you like, but the company's minimum is too high, do not give up. Most companies have automatic investment plans that are very flexible. For example: You want to invest in ABC fund. The minimum initial investment is $250 and additional contributions must be $100 or more. You can only save $50 per month. All you need to do is save $50 per month until the minimum initial investment of $250 is reached. Once you have the minimum initial investment, sign up for their automatic payment plan. The automatic payment plan will withdraw money from your bank account (or payroll) at regular intervals. If you want to invest $50 per month and the minimum additional contributions are $100, have the automatic payments withdraw $100 every other month. You save $50 a month, in 2 months you will have the $100.

Review what the fund companies have to offer and the expenses of each fund. Read the prospectus (information about the fund) and click on "application." You will have a choice of filling the application out on-line, printing the application on your printer and mailing it in, or having the application mailed to you. Call the fund company if you need assistance. The fund companies telephone representatives are friendly and helpful. Never worry about feeling embarrassed about asking a question. It is your money and they are there to help.

Typical information needed to fill out a mutual fund IRA application:

Section one—Your full name, social security number, date of birth, address, and phone number.

Section two—Your beneficiary's full name, social security number, date of birth, address, and phone number.

Section three—Your fund selection and the initial investment.

Section four—Which type of IRA are you investing in? Traditional or Roth? Which year are you investing in? The year you are investing in is usually the current year. However, if you have not invested in an IRA for the previous year and it is currently before the tax deadline in April, you may contribute for the previous year. You would want to do this because the maximums that you are allowed to invest in an IRA yearly. If you start in the previous year, it doesn't affect your contributions for this year. Let's say it is January and you want to start this IRA with $250. If you submit the $250 for the previous year, you can still put the maximum contribution this year into the IRA.

Section five—When you start withdrawing money from your IRA (hopefully this is 30+ years from now), do you want the fund company to withhold income taxes or do you want to deal with the taxes yourself?

Section six—Are you going to have money automatically deposited into your IRA? You need to enter the monthly amount and days you would like it withdrawn. The fund company will also require you to send a voided check to get your proper routing number for your bank.

Section seven—Your signature. Just like the IRS, they cannot process your paperwork without it.

How To Track Your Investments

This is a sample of what you would find in the business section of most newspapers. Once you know what all of the figures are for, it is very simple to track your investment.

First, go to the list of mutual funds in the business section. Second, find your Family of Funds (example: Strong Funds, Invesco Funds, T. Rowe Price Funds, etc...). Third, find your specific fund listed under your fund family. Now, what do all of those numbers mean?

Let us pretend that Basicinvest is a mutual fund company and one of the funds that they offer is the Index 500 fund. The listing in the paper would look like this:

	NAV	CHG	PCT CHG	1-YR RTN	3-YR RTN
Basicinvest					
Idx 500	24.34	+.07	+.29	9.8	21.4

NAV (Net Asset Value) is the share price. One share of this fund is $24.34. If you buy $250 worth of this fund, you would have 10.271 shares.

CHG (change) is the price increase or decrease. The Basicinvest Index 500 Fund increased 7 cents a share.

PCT CHG (percent change) is the percent the share price changed for the day.

1-YR RTN (1 year return) is the return percent increase or decrease for the last 12 months. This fund has increased 9.8% in the last 12 months.

3-YR RTN (3 year return) is the return percent increase or decrease averaged out for the last 3 years. This fund has averaged 21.4% each year for the past 3 years.

Every year you should review your portfolio to make sure the funds are performing up to your expectations. Check the performance of your funds. If your fund is consistently under performing other funds that invest in the same type of companies, you may want to switch funds.

You should also review your asset allocation yearly. Your portfolio may contain bonds and stock funds. According to your risk tolerance, you want the portfolio to be 20% bonds and 80% stocks. If the stock market returns significantly outpace the bond returns, your bond allocation will decrease and your stock allocation will increase. You will have to move money from your stock fund into bonds to bring your bond allocation back up to 20%.

CONCLUSIONS

Hopefully you have:
1. Set-up your budget
2. Reduced or eliminated your debt
3. Have an Emergency Fund

Once these 3 things are done, the only thing stopping you from investing is YOU. Get started!

Appendix A:
Power of Compounding Charts

All figures are assuming money is contributed into a tax deferred account (example: Roth IRA) and all dividends and gains reinvested.

Investment of $50 per month

	2%	5%	13%	15%
Years				
20	$14,740	20,550	56,660	74,861
30	24,630	41,610	218,660	346,163
40	36,730	76,300	808,950	1,550,800

Investment of $100 per month

Years	2%	5%	13%	15%
20	$29,470	41,100	113,320	149,720
30	49,270	83,220	437,320	692,320
40	73,443	152,600	1,617,900	3,101,600

Investment of $166 per month ($2000/year into IRA)

	2%	5%	13%	15%
Years				
20	$48,930	68,230	188,110	248,540
30	81,790	138,150	725,960	1.149,260
40	121,910	253,310	2,685,724	5,148,665

Investment of $200 per month

Years	2%	5%	13%	15%
20	$58,950	82,200	226,640	299,440
30	98,540	166,450	874,650	1,384,655
40	146,880	305,200	3,235,900	6,203,210

Investment of $250 per month ($3000/year into IRA)

Years	2%	5%	13%	15%
20	$73,700	102,750	283,310	374,300
30	123,180	208,060	1,093,317	1,730,810
40	183,600	381,505	4,044,766	7,754,010

Investment of $333 per month
($2000/year into your IRA, $2000/year into spouses IRA)

Years	2%	5%	13%	15%
20	$98,167	136,870	377,360	498,580
30	164,070	277,142	1,456,290	2,305,450
40	244,560	508,164	5,387,620	10,328,346

APPENDIX B:
EASY-TO-UNDERSTAND DEFINITIONS

Some definitions are under the "Spotlight." These definitions are expanded and described in more detail. Each definition is listed alphabetically and each spotlighted definition is separated by its own page.

12b-1 Fee

A fee charged by some mutual funds to cover promotion and marketing expenses.

401(k) Plan

An employer-sponsored account, which allows employees to set aside tax deferred income for retirement purposes. The name 401(k) comes from the IRS section describing the program.

403(b) Plan

A retirement plan similar to a 401k, but is offered by non-profit organizations.

Spotlight

529 College Savings Plan

College savings plans allow you to open an account for a child, grandchild, or other young person. Some have no maximum annual contribution.

Qualified withdrawals are tax free.

Earnings are tax-deferred.

And a reassuring benefit to many parents is that the account owner controls the money until it's used for college.

You could transfer the account to another family member with anticipated college expenses (including yourself).

The new law also lets you transfer accounts between cousins. You could even take the money back for another purpose, although the earnings would then be taxable and you'd pay a penalty equal to 10% of earnings.

American Stock Exchange (AMEX)

The second largest stock exchange in the U.S., after the New York Stock Exchange (NYSE). Stocks and bonds traded on the AMEX tend to be those of smaller companies than those on the NYSE.

Annual Return

The increase or decrease in value of an investment expressed as a percentage per year and taking into consideration the effects of compounding.

Spotlight

Annuity

A contract sold by an insurance company designed to provide payments to the holder at specified intervals. All funds in the annuity grow tax deferred. An early withdrawal penalty often applies. When you buy a single-premium immediate annuity, you receive fixed monthly checks for life or for a specified period. There are other annuities that are similar to traditional IRA's. Because of the complexity of annuities, policies, expenses, etc...It is highly advisable to contact a Certified Financial Planner to evaluate your situation to see if annuities are a good choice for you. To find out more about annuities on the internet, you can visit www.tiaa-cref.org.

Asset

Any item of economic value owned by an individual or corporation.

Asset Allocation

Percentage allocated to different types of investments (cash, stocks, bonds, etc...) for diversification purposes.

Asset Allocation Fund

A single mutual fund which accomplishes the goal of asset allocation all by itself.

Automatic Investment Plan

A program that allows an individual to have a set amount electronically transferred from one account to another at a specified frequency (also see Dollar Cost Averaging).

Back-end Load

A sales charge (commission) paid when an individual sells an investment. Intended to discourage withdrawals.

Balanced Fund

A mutual fund that buys a combination of stocks and bonds to provide both income and capital appreciation while avoiding excessive risk.

Spotlight

Bear Market

A prolonged period of falling prices, usually by 15% or more, accompanied by widespread pessimism. Do not let the pessimism scare you. If you are:

Investing for the long term

Dollar cost averaging

Happy with your investments up to this point

Ride it out. Some newer investors may get scared and sell their stock or funds only to regret it later. If you are losing sleep over it, you probably should not have been invested in such a volatile investment. Try to ride it out then sell and buy something more conservative.

Spotlight

Blue Chip

A large, national company with a solid record of stable earnings and/or dividend growth and a reputation for high quality personnel and products. Because of size and reputation of these companies, they are usually less risky than other stocks.

The name Blue Chip came from poker. Blue poker chips are usually the more expensive ones.

You will find Blue Chip stocks in the S&P 500 and list of Dow Jones Industrials

Bond

Interest bearing certificate used for income.

Bond Fund

A mutual fund, which invests in bonds, typically with the goal of providing stable income with minimal risk.

Broker

An individual or firm which acts as a "middle-man" between a buyer and seller of investments, usually charging a commission.

Budget

An itemized list of total expenses vs. total income, then setting aside a specified amount regularly.

Spotlight

Bull Market

A prolonged period of rising prices, usually by 20% or more. Bargain stocks and mutual funds become harder to find during a bull market because prices are usually higher. Investors become optimistic and sometimes venture into riskier investments that they normally would not invest in. Evaluate your risk tolerance and do not let your emotions guide your investment decisions..

Business Cycle

A semi-predictable pattern of alternating periods of economic growth and decline.

Spotlight

Buy and Hold

One of the most successful ways of investing. A strategy in which investments are bought and then held for a long period, regardless of the market's fluctuations. The buy and hold approach should focus on selecting high quality companies with a history of above average returns and dividends. By accumulating these investments selectively over time and holding them, an investor minimizes transaction costs while maximizing the possibility of enjoying the long-term returns generated from the investment.

Call

An option contract that gives the holder the right to buy a certain quantity of an underlying security from the writer of the option, at a specified price up to a specified date.

Call Price

The price at which a bond or preferred stock can be redeemed by the issuer.

Capital Gain

The amount by which an asset's selling price exceeds its initial purchase price.

Spotlight

Capital Gains Distribution

A capital gain is when the fund manager sells a stock in the fund for a profit. The profit (gain) is distributed to the shareholders. The shareholders will have to pay taxes on the distribution. For example: you buy a mutual fund at $40 per share. The mutual fund distributes a $4 per share gain to its shareholders. The share price will drop by the distribution amount ($40 per share will drop to $36) and the shareholder pays tax on the $4 per share. If you purchase the fund before the distribution record date, you will pay taxes on the distribution as if you had the fund all year.

There is not a required month that all mutual funds must distribute their capital gains. However, most distribute their gains October through December. If you purchase shares in September and the funds distribution date is in October, you may end up paying capital gains on that fund for the entire tax year even though you had the fund only one month. What to do? Call or e-mail the fund company and ask for the distribution record date for that specific fund.

Capitalization

The total value of stocks and bonds outstanding of a corporation.

Certificate of Deposit (CD)

Interest bearing certificate offered by banks and savings and loans, usually 3 month to 5 year terms. Low risk, low return (typically 3% to 6%). There is usually an early withdrawal penalty.

Spotlight

Certified Financial Planner (CFP)

CFP's must pass a comprehensive exam that tests their personal financial planning knowledge and skills, continually update their abilities and abide by the CFP Board's Code of Ethics and Professional Responsibility and Financial Planning Practice Standards. When searching for a CFP, try to find one that is fee-based. This means that that will charge based on an hourly rate, a flat rate, or on a percentage of your assets and/or income. Some questions you may ask: What experience do you have, what are your qualifications, what services do you offer, what is your approach to financial planning, will you be the only person working with me, how will I pay for your services, how much do you charge, have you ever been disciplined publicly for unlawful or unethical behavior, can I get everything in writing?

The official CFP boards web site is www.cfp-board.org. You can look up the CFP's certification, check up on a planner, and get free information.

Certified Public Accountant (CPA)

An individual who has received state certification to practice accounting.

Chartered Financial Analyst (CFA)

An individual who has passed tests in economics, accounting, investment analysis, and money management administered by the Institute of Chartered Financial Analysts.

Chartered Financial Consultant (ChFC)

An individual who has completed a program of economics, taxes, insurance, and investing.

Chartered Life Underwriter (CLU)

An individual who has completed training in life insurance and personal insurance planning.

Spotlight

Commission

A fee or "load" charged by a broker for his/her service in facilitating a transaction, such as the buying or selling of stocks. Why is this important? You want to purchase a mutual fund at $50 per share. Your initial investment is $10,000. You complete some very good research and find two similar funds taht have very similar holdings. Their expenses are the same except one has a 4.75% load and one is no-load.

$50 per share times 4.75% load = you pay 52.375 per share. $10,000 would buy 190.931 shares

$50 per share, no-load = $50 per share. $10,000 would buy 200 shares

You lost money and you haven't even started investing. I am not saying that the load should be your deciding factor, however in this case where two funds are the same, go with the no-load.

Common Stock

Equity ownership in a corporation with voting rights and entitling the holder to a share of the company's dividends and/or capital appreciation/depreciation.

Compounding

A process whereby the value of an investment increases over time due to compound interest.

Compound Interest

Interest which is calculated not only on the initial principal, but also the accumulated interest of prior periods.

Custodial Account (also see UGMA and UTMA)

An account opened on the behalf of a minor by an adult who acts as custodian. The custodian is usually one of the child's parents. Any assets placed into a custodial account are irrevocable. Once the minor is of maturity (usually 18, but some states are 21), they may do what they please with the assets.

Day Order

A buy or sell order which automatically expires if it is not executed during that trading session.

Debt

A liability owed to another person or persons and required to be paid by a specified date.

Debt/Equity Ratio

A measure of a company's leverage, calculated by dividing long-term debt by common shareholders equity.

Diamonds

Shares representing all 30 stocks in the Dow Jones Industrial Average. Traded on the American Stock Exchange.

Discount Brokerage

A brokerage which offers lower commission rates than a full service brokerage for the purchase and selling of investments. Discount brokerages usually provide less "human" assistance with your trades and portfolio.

Distribution

The payment of a dividend or capital gain.

Diversification

Owning investments that are not in the same industry or business for the purpose of reducing risk.

Spotlight

Dividend

A taxable payment declared by a company's board of directors and given to its shareholders out of the company's current or retained profits. Dividends add to the total return of stocks. Stocks paying high dividends become more attractive during down markets. Many high dividend stocks tend to be more conservative investments like banks, energy, and real estate companies.

Dollar Cost Averaging

Designed to reduce volatility in which securities are purchased in fixed dollar amounts at regular intervals, regardless of what direction the market is moving. See chapter in the book. Also see definitions:

Automatic Investment Plan

Compounding

Buy and Hold

Spotlight

Dow Jones Industrial Average (DJIA)

The most widely used indicator of the overall condition of the stock market. A price-weighted average of 30 actively traded blue chip stocks. The Dow Jones industrial average is calculated by adding up the current prices of the 30 stocks that make up the index and dividing by a special divisor.

The divisor started out as the number of stocks in the index, but the divisor has been adjusted when a stock in the industrial average splits its shares, or when a company is added or removed from the index. This helps maintain the index's continuity.

Spotlight

Education Saving Account (Education IRA)

Tax-deferred financial planning vehicle, which enables a person to save money for future education-related expenses. Starting in 2002, maximum contributions are $2000 and you can contribute to both Education Savings Accounts and qualified tuition programs (529 plans) in the same year for the same beneficiary. The new phase-out range for married couples filing jointly is $190,000 to $220,000 of modified Adjusted Gross Income (AGI). For single filers, the phase-out range remains at $95,000 to $110,000 of modified Adjusted Gross Income.

Qualified expenses for Education Savings Accounts will include: The purchase of any computer technology or equipment if the services are to be used by the beneficiary during any of the years the beneficiary is in school. Room and board, uniforms, transportation, and supplementary items or services (including extended day programs) required or provided by such a school in connection with enrollment. Tuition, fees, academic tutoring, special needs services, books, supplies, and other equipment incurred with the enrollment or attendance of the beneficiary at a public, private, or religious school providing elementary or secondary education (kindergarten through grade 12), as well as college

Emergency Fund

Easily accessible cash for use in case of an unexpected expense (usually 2 to 6 months of your salary).

Equities

Same as stock.

Equity Fund

A mutual fund which invests primarily in stocks.

Exchange Traded Fund (ETF)

A fund that tracks an index, but can be traded like a stock.

Expense Ratio

A mutual fund's operating expenses, expressed as a percentage of its average net assets. Higher expenses reduce your funds overall total return.

Front-end Load

A sales charge paid when an individual buys an investment.

Fund Manager

The individual responsible for making portfolio decisions.

Spotlight

Gift Tax

A tax against a person who gives money, or an asset, to another person without receiving fair compensation. In 2002 you could give as many people as you wished annual gifts of $11,000 each without triggering the federal gift tax. If both spouses joined in the gift, you could give away $22,000 to each of your children. Besides giving your kids a financial head start, making a gift can also be an attractive estate-planning tool for parents (and grandparents) who would like to distribute assets from their estate before they die. Unlike charitable donations, gifts to individuals can't be deducted on your return.

Growth and Income Fund

A mutual fund investing in companies which have earnings growth as well as dividends.

Growth Fund

A mutual fund whose aim is to achieve capital appreciation by investing in growth stocks.

Hedge Fund

A fund which is allowed to use strategies that are unavailable to mutual funds, including selling short, leveraging, program trading, etc...Very high minimum investment.

Income Fund

A mutual fund which emphasizes current income.

Index

A benchmark in which financial or economic performance is measured.

Index Fund

A mutual that tries to mirror the performance of a specific index, such as the S&P 500. Since transactions are infrequent, expenses tend to be lower than those of actively managed funds.

Individual Account

Account set up for one person.

Individual Retirement Account (IRA)

A tax-deferred retirement account that permits individuals to set aside money until withdrawals begin at age 59 ½ or later.

Spotlight

Inflation

The overall general upward price of goods and services in an economy, usually as measured by the Consumer Price Index and the Producer Price Index. Inflation should be factored into all of your financial plans. If you are 25 years old and feel you could retire comfortably with a nest egg of one million dollars, if you do not factor in inflation, you may be in a lot of trouble. At age 65 averaging a 3% rate of inflation, you would need over $3,000,000 to match your $1,000,000 today. How about college costs? Planning for your child? College costs are rising at the rate of 5% per year. One year of private college is averaging over $16,000. If your child is one and you start an investment account averaging 10%, if you do not account for the 5% yearly increase, you would contribute $115 per month into their account until age 18 to cover college costs. When your child turned 18, you would have a big surprise. You would be several thousands of dollars short. If you added the 5% inflation factor every year, you would need to contribute $285 per month at age one to cover college costs.

Initial Public Offering (IPO)

The first sale of stock by a company to the public.

Interest

The fee charged by a lender to a borrower for the use of the borrowed money, usually expressed as an annual percentage of the principal.

International Fund

A mutual fund which invests in stocks and bonds of companies mostly outside of the U.S.

Investment

An item of value purchased for income or capital appreciation.

Joint Account

An account that is owned jointly by two or more clients.

Large Cap

Over $5 billion capitalization.

Leverage

The degree to which an investor or business is utilizing borrowed money.

Limit Order

An order to a broker to buy a specified quantity of a security at or below a specified price, or to sell it at or above a specified price.

Load (also see Commission)

A sales charge added to the purchase and/or sale price of some mutual funds and annuities.

Management Fee

A charge paid to a mutual fund's managers for their services; usually also includes fund administration costs and investor relations. Usually a certain percentage of assets under management.

Margin Account

An account in which the brokerage company lends the customer cash with which to purchase securities.

Market Order

A buy or sell order in which the broker is to execute the order at the best price currently available.

Market Timing

Attempting to predict future market direction and investing based on those predictions. Usually a very unsuccessful way of investing.

Maturity

The date on which a debt becomes due for payment.

Mid Cap

$1 billion to $5 billion capitalization.

Money Market Account (MMA)

Designed for current income. Typically safe, easily accessible investments. Returns usually range from 3% to 6%.

Mutual Fund

Invests in a group of assets (stocks, bonds, cash) and traded as shares in accordance with a stated set of objectives. Benefits include diversification and professional money management.

NASDAQ

National Association of Securities Dealers Automated Quotations system.

Net Asset Value (NAV)

The dollar value of a single mutual fund share, based on the value of the underlying assets of the fund minus its liabilities, divided by the number of shares outstanding.

No-load

Without any sales charge.

NYSE

New York Stock Exchange.

Option

The option, but not the obligation, to buy or sell a specific amount of a given stock, commodity, currency, index, or debt, at a specified price during a specified period of time.

Overvalued

Perceived to be too expensive.

Spotlight

Pension Plan

A qualified retirement plan set up by a corporation, labor union, government, or other organization for its employees. Depending on your company's pension plan rules, you may be eligible for a pension after a period of service (see plan administrator) known as the vesting period. However, not all workers or all jobs may be included. Most company pension plan benefits are paid out in the form of an annuity, a fixed monthly payment for the rest of your life. The formula used to calculate company pension plan benefits typically includes your final salary, years of service, and a fixed percentage rate. When you leave your job, your pension benefits stay in the company-sponsored plan, where they can be claimed at age 65. Some pension plans allow you to begin collecting pension benefits before the traditional retirement age of 65. However, like Social Security, your benefit may be reduced because you will be receiving benefits over a longer period of time.

Spotlight

Price to Earnings ratio (P/E ratio)

Equal to a stock's capitalization divided by its after-tax earnings over a 12-month period. An indicator of a stock's value. The P/E ratio provides insight into an investment using an easily understood yardstick: earnings. Stocks with high P/Es compared to the overall market are typically growth stocks. Investors are willing to pay a premium because they expect the company's stock price to rise. Stocks with low P/Es are sometimes considered overlooked value stocks. Because earnings are volatile, the P/E has its limitations and may fail as a measure for a significant number of stocks at any given time.

Prospectus

A legal document that is an offer to sell securities. The document pro-vides useful information in making informed investment decisions. This book contains detailed information about a prospectus. You are required to read the funds prospectus before investing the fund.

Put

An option contract that gives the holder the right to sell a certain quan-tity of an underlying security to the writer of the option, at a specified price up to a specified date.

Spotlight

Real Estate Investment Trust (REIT)

Invests the shareholders money in real estate and loans for real estate development. A REIT is a company dedicated to owning and, in most cases, operating income-producing real estate, such as apartments, shopping centers, offices and warehouses. Some REITs also are engaged in financing real estate.

The current average dividend yield for a REIT is 8.0%. REITs offer the most efficient and economical method of real estate ownership. REITs are not for everyone, but they can play a role in you diversification plans. To be a REIT, a company is legally required to pay virtually all of its taxable income (90 percent) to its shareholders every year. Since their inception, REITs have provided competitive investment performance. In recent years and over the long-term, REIT market performance has been roughly comparable to that of the Russell 2000 Index and has exceeded returns on fixed debt instruments or direct investments in real estate.

Most mutual fund companies offer a REIT fund. Examine each fund just as if you were buying another type of stock mutual fund. Do not forget to read the fund prospectus..

Spotlight

Recession

A period of general economic decline for two or more consecutive quarters. Recessions are usually associated with periods of declining employment as well as output. When output is declining, firms have less need to employ workers, and this translates to fewer people employed and a rise in the unemployment rate.

Recessions can be of various durations. Since 1945, the average recession has lasted 11 months.

Just the word Recession can spread fear into investors. In turn, the more inexperienced investor will pull their money out of the stock market and place it into a more secure Money Market or CD. Even if a recession is not actually occuring at the time, this wide spread panic could make the stock market drop by hundreds in a single day.

Registered Investment Adviser (RIA)

Registered advisor with the security exchange commission. No certification is required.

Reinvest

Using the profits, dividends, or interest from an investment to buy more of that investment.

Return

The annual return on an investment, expressed as a percentage of the total amount invested.

Return On Investment (ROI)

A measure of a corporation's profitability, equal to a fiscal year's income divided by common stock and preferred stock equity plus long-term debt.

Risk

The quantifiable likelihood of loss.

Risk Tolerance

An investor's ability to handle declines in the value of his/her portfolio.

Rollover

A tax-free reinvestment of a distribution from a qualified retirement plan (401k, 403b, etc…) into an IRA or other qualified plan within 60 days.

Roth IRA

Allows taxpayers to save for retirement while allowing the savings to grow tax-free. Taxes are paid on contributions, but withdrawals are not taxed at all.

S&P 500

A composite index that tracks 500 industrial, transportation, public utility, and financial stocks.

Sector Fund

A mutual fund that invests in the stocks of a particular industry.

Securities and Exchange Commission (SEC)

The primary federal regulatory agency for the securities industry. The responsibility of the SEC is to promote full disclosure and to protect investors against fraudulent and manipulative practices.

Share

Certificate representing one unit of ownership in a corporation, mutual fund, or limited partnership.

Small Cap

$250 million to $1 billion capitalization.

Spotlight

Split

You do not loose or gain anything when a stock splits (common misconception). A split is completed to make a stock, with a very high per-share price, more accessible to small investors. For example: if you own 100 shares of XYZ selling at $60 per share (100 X $60= $6000). After the split you will have twice the amount of shares at half the price (200 X $30= $6000).

Some believe that when a stock splits, it makes the stock more attractive, people will purchase more shares, and in turn the price will go up. In a bull market, this may be the case, however it is usually temporary. Unless you can predict exactly when you believe the company will announce the split and exactly when it will peak right after the split, I would suggest not to purchase a stock solely because it is going to split.

Stock

An instrument that signifies an ownership in a corporation and represents a claim on its proportionate share in the corporation's assets and profits.

Tax-deferred

Income whose taxes can be postponed until a later date. You may own a mutual fund in a Traditional IRA. Even though the fund had a capital gains distribution this year, you will not have to pay taxes on the gain until you start withdrawing money at retirement.

Tax-efficient

Having less of a tax consequence than other similar investments.

Spotlight

Turnover

The number of shares traded for a period as a percentage of the total shares. High turnover may effect your after-tax returns due to capital gains. These days, the turnover ratio for the average stock fund is around 100 percent, indicating that all of the fund's securities were bought and sold within one year's time. Higher turnover eats into your profits through short-term capital gains. If you like a fund that has high turnover, think about placing that fund in your Roth IRA. this will save you money by not paying the high taxes on the fund. Because fund manager's must pass along the capital gains to its holders, you may be able to find a tax efficient manger that sells securities at a loss to offset gains.

Spotlight

Uniform Gift to Minors Act (UGMA) and Transfer to Minors Act (UTMA)

Laws adopted by most states allowing an adult to contribute to a custodial account in a minor's name. These have become less attractive since the new 2002 Education IRA and 529 Plan changes. Do not rule them out just yet. Starting in 2002, you can only contribute $2000 to an Education IRA and 529 Plans are limited to the plan administrators investments, which may be below the stock market average of 13%. You may want to invest in all three investment tools to maximize your diversity anf tax efficiency.

If the child begins college before reaching the age when the custodianship ends, money in an UGMA or UTMA can be used to pay higher education costs, as long as the custodian agrees. When the child reaches the age when custodianship terminates, however, he or she takes complete control of the assets and can use them for any purpose. There is no limit to the amount of money that can be invested in an UGMA or UTMA, so you can use it to cover a significant portion of your child's college costs. Because the first $700 dollars of *earnings* are not taxed, and a child's tax rate is usually lower than an adult's, UGMAs and UTMAs can produce significant tax savings for your family. (A child under 14 will pay tax at their parents' rate on investment income greater than $1,400.) The greater the difference between the child's tax rate and the parents', the greater the benefit of the UGMA/UTMA.

Value Stock

A stock that is considered to be a good stock at a great price, based on its fundamentals.

Variable Annuity

An annuity contract which provides future payments to the holder usually at retirement, the size of which depends on the performance of the portfolio's securities (see annuity).

Yield

The annual rate of return on an investment, expressed as a percentage. For securities, it is the annual dividends divided by the purchase price.

APPENDIX C:
MUTUAL FUND COMPANIES AND
HELPFUL WEB SITES

To qualify for minimum initial investment, you may have to sign up for an IRA and/or automatic investment plan. Read company prospectus before investing. Minimums change frequently, ask representative current minimum for specific fund.

Name	Minimum Initial Investment	Phone Number
AARP	$500	1-800-253-2277
Babson	$100	1-800-422-2766
Fidelity	$500	1-800-544-6666
Gabelli	$0	1-800-422-3554
Invesco	$50	1-800-675-1705
T. Rowe Price	$50	1-800-638-5660
Janus	$500	1-800-525-3713

Pax World	$250	1-800-767-1729
Stein Roe	$500	1-800-338-2550
Strong	$250	1-800-359-3329
Tiaa-Cref	$25	1-800-842-7782
The Vanguard Group	$1000	1-800-871-3879

Helpful Free Web Sites

www.basicinvest.com

www.estrong.com

www.tiaa-cref.org

www.vanguard.com

Appendix D:
Mutual Fund Review Forms

Use these forms to help you compare funds. The fund companies internet site should contain all of the information or call the company on the phone for the answers. There are several copies so you can use some forms now and some later, if you decide to add funds to your portfolio.

Example of filled out form
Mutual Fund Company: *Basicinvest*

Fund Name: *S&P 500 Index*

Funds Objective: _*Long term growth and Income*___ Is this an Income fund? Growth fund? Does the fund invest in Small-caps or Large-caps?

Funds Top Ten Holdings: GE, IBM, Coke, Walmart, Exxon, Microsoft, Pfizer, Citigroup, Intel, AIG

Does the fund invest in companies that you are familiar with? Have you heard of any of these companies? YES

Funds Annual Performance: 10 year 13%, 5 year 11%, 3 year 5%, 1 year 5%

How long has the fund manager been with the fund? 8 years. **If the fund manager started last week, the prior annual performance stats may not mean much.**

Is the fund No-load? __Y___

If the fund has a Load, what is the percent? _____

What are the total expenses of the fund? .2 **A few percentage points add up to a lot over 20 or 30 years. If you find similar funds, go with the lower expenses.**

Mutual Fund Company: _____

Fund Name: _____

Funds Objective: _____

Funds Top Ten Holdings: _____, _____, _____, _____, _____, _____, _____, _____, _____, _____

Does the fund invest in companies that you are familiar with? Have you heard of any of these companies?

Funds Annual Performance: 10 year _____, 5 year _____, 3 year _____, 1 year _____

How long has the fund manager been with the fund? _____

Is the fund No-load? _____

If the fund has a Load, what is the percent? _____

What are the total expenses of the fund? _____

Mutual Fund Company: _____

Fund Name: _____

Funds Objective: _____

Funds Top Ten Holdings: _____, _____, _____, _____, _____, _____, _____, _____, _____, _____

Does the fund invest in companies that you are familiar with? Have you heard of any of these companies?

Funds Annual Performance: 10 year _____, 5 year _____, 3 year _____, 1 year _____

How long has the fund manager been with the fund? _____

Is the fund No-load? _____

If the fund has a Load, what is the percent? _____

What are the total expenses of the fund? _____

Mutual Fund Company: _____

Fund Name: _____

Funds Objective: _____

Funds Top Ten Holdings: _____, _____, _____, _____, _____, _____, _____, _____, _____, _____

Does the fund invest in companies that you are familiar with? Have you heard of any of these companies?

Funds Annual Performance: 10 year _____, 5 year _____, 3 year _____, 1 year _____

How long has the fund manager been with the fund? _____

Is the fund No-load? _____

If the fund has a Load, what is the percent? _____

What are the total expenses of the fund? _____

Mutual Fund Company: _____

Fund Name: _____

Funds Objective: _____

Funds Top Ten Holdings: _____, _____, _____, _____, _____, _____, _____, _____, _____, _____

Does the fund invest in companies that you are familiar with? Have you heard of any of these companies?

Funds Annual Performance: 10 year _____, 5 year _____, 3 year _____, 1 year _____

How long has the fund manager been with the fund? _____

Is the fund No-load? _____

If the fund has a Load, what is the percent? _____

What are the total expenses of the fund? _____

Mutual Fund Company: _____

Fund Name: _____

Funds Objective: _____

Funds Top Ten Holdings: _____, _____, _____, _____, _____, _____, _____, _____, _____, _____

Does the fund invest in companies that you are familiar with? Have you heard of any of these companies?

Funds Annual Performance: 10 year _____, 5 year _____, 3 year _____, 1 year _____

How long has the fund manager been with the fund? _____

Is the fund No-load? _____

If the fund has a Load, what is the percent? _____

What are the total expenses of the fund? _____

Mutual Fund Company: _____

Fund Name: _____

Funds Objective: _____

Funds Top Ten Holdings: _____, _____, _____, _____, _____, _____, _____, _____, _____, _____

Does the fund invest in companies that you are familiar with? Have you heard of any of these companies?

Funds Annual Performance: 10 year _____, 5 year _____, 3 year _____, 1 year _____

How long has the fund manager been with the fund? _____

Is the fund No-load? _____

If the fund has a Load, what is the percent? _____

What are the total expenses of the fund? _____

Mutual Fund Company: _____

Fund Name: _____

Funds Objective: _____

Funds Top Ten Holdings: _____, _____, _____, _____, _____, _____, _____, _____, _____, _____

Does the fund invest in companies that you are familiar with? Have you heard of any of these companies?

Funds Annual Performance: 10 year _____, 5 year _____, 3 year _____, 1 year _____

How long has the fund manager been with the fund? _____

Is the fund No-load? _____

If the fund has a Load, what is the percent? _____

What are the total expenses of the fund? _____

Mutual Fund Company: _____

Fund Name: _____

Funds Objective: _____

Funds Top Ten Holdings: _____, _____, _____, _____, _____, _____, _____, _____, _____, _____

Does the fund invest in companies that you are familiar with? Have you heard of any of these companies?

Funds Annual Performance: 10 year _____, 5 year _____, 3 year _____, 1 year _____

How long has the fund manager been with the fund? _____

Is the fund No-load? _____

If the fund has a Load, what is the percent? _____

What are the total expenses of the fund? _____

Mutual Fund Company: _____

Fund Name: _____

Funds Objective: _____

Funds Top Ten Holdings: _____, _____, _____, _____, _____, _____, _____, _____, _____, _____

Does the fund invest in companies that you are familiar with? Have you heard of any of these companies?

Funds Annual Performance: 10 year _____, 5 year _____, 3 year _____, 1 year _____

How long has the fund manager been with the fund? _____

Is the fund No-load? _____

If the fund has a Load, what is the percent? _____

What are the total expenses of the fund? _____

Mutual Fund Company: _____

Fund Name: _____

Funds Objective: _____

Funds Top Ten Holdings: _____, _____, _____, _____, _____, _____, _____, _____, _____, _____

Does the fund invest in companies that you are familiar with? Have you heard of any of these companies?

Funds Annual Performance: 10 year _____, 5 year _____, 3 year _____, 1 year _____

How long has the fund manager been with the fund? _____

Is the fund No-load? _____

If the fund has a Load, what is the percent? _____

What are the total expenses of the fund? _____

Mutual Fund Company: _____

Fund Name: _____

Funds Objective: _____

Funds Top Ten Holdings: _____, _____, _____,
_____, _____, _____, _____, _____,
_____, _____

Does the fund invest in companies that you are familiar with? Have you heard of any of these companies?

Funds Annual Performance: 10 year _____, 5 year _____, 3 year _____,
1 year _____

How long has the fund manager been with the fund? _____

Is the fund No-load? _____

If the fund has a Load, what is the percent? _____

What are the total expenses of the fund? _____

Mutual Fund Company: _____

Fund Name: _____

Funds Objective: _____

Funds Top Ten Holdings: _____, _____, _____,
_____, _____, _____, _____, _____,
_____, _____

Does the fund invest in companies that you are familiar with? Have you heard of any of these companies?

Funds Annual Performance: 10 year _____, 5 year _____, 3 year _____, 1 year _____

How long has the fund manager been with the fund? _____

Is the fund No-load? _____

If the fund has a Load, what is the percent? _____

What are the total expenses of the fund? _____

Mutual Fund Company: _____

Fund Name: _____

Funds Objective: _____

Funds Top Ten Holdings: _____, _____, _____, _____, _____, _____, _____, _____, _____, _____

Does the fund invest in companies that you are familiar with? Have you heard of any of these companies?

Funds Annual Performance: 10 year _____, 5 year _____, 3 year _____, 1 year _____

How long has the fund manager been with the fund? _____

Is the fund No-load? _____

If the fund has a Load, what is the percent? _____

What are the total expenses of the fund? _____

Mutual Fund Company: _____

Fund Name: _____

Funds Objective: _____

Funds Top Ten Holdings: _____, _____, _____,
_____, _____, _____, _____, _____,
_____, _____

Does the fund invest in companies that you are familiar with? Have you
heard of any of these companies?

Funds Annual Performance: 10 year _____, 5 year _____, 3 year _____,
1 year _____

How long has the fund manager been with the fund? _____

Is the fund No-load? _____

If the fund has a Load, what is the percent? _____

What are the total expenses of the fund? _____

Mutual Fund Company: _____

Fund Name: _____

Funds Objective: _____

Funds Top Ten Holdings: _____, _____, _____, _____, _____, _____, _____, _____, _____, _____

Does the fund invest in companies that you are familiar with? Have you heard of any of these companies?

Funds Annual Performance: 10 year _____, 5 year _____, 3 year _____, 1 year _____

How long has the fund manager been with the fund? _____

Is the fund No-load? _____

If the fund has a Load, what is the percent? _____

What are the total expenses of the fund? _____

0-595-21183-6

www.ingramcontent.com/pod-product-compliance
Lightning Source LLC
Chambersburg PA
CBHW030839180526
45163CB00004B/1382